One Needle, One Treatment
一根针，一种治疗

Written and illustrated by Prof. Jin Ke Yu
Executive Director
World Association of Chinese Medicine (Beijing)

金科煜教授
（世界中医学会执行理事）
撰写并插图

W9-BBA-047

Foreign Languages Press

First Edition   2006

Home Page:
  http://www.flp.com.cn
E-mail Addresses:
  info@flp.com.cn
  sales@flp.com.cn

ISBN 7-119-04441-9
© Foreign Languages Press, Beijing, China, 2006
Published by Foreign Languages Press
24 Baiwanzhuang Road, Beijing 100037, China

Distributed by China International Book Trading Corporation
35 Chegongzhuang Xilu, Beijing 100044, China
P.O. Box 399, Beijing, China
Printed in the People's Republic of China

Acupuncture is a means of perturbing the latent energy (Qi) of a living creature with the assistance of needles implanted into the body, in order to restore the natural balance of Qi and promote health.

Knowledge of Acupuncture is still limited because the practitioner is often afraid of its complex theory and the manipulation of the universal Qi through the magnificent corridor of life.

This book hopes to make the ancient art of acupuncture more accessible to the general practitioner by describing the treatment of a number of common ailments which involve the use of only one needle.

针灸是一种借助于向体内进行针刺来刺激体内能量（气），恢复人体能量的自然平衡，从而保持健康的方法。

目前人们对针灸的知识还很有限，执业者也往往感到其理论的深邃和复杂，如何在神奇的生命脉络中操纵和疏导宇宙之气，则为历代执业者所孜孜以求。

本书旨在通过介绍一些常见病的医治，使这门只用一根针的古老医术更易于为广大执业者所掌握。

CONTENTS
目 录

1. Acute Lumbar Pain

Point: 人中/水沟
Renzhong — GV 26

Particularity:
Opens the orifices to induce resuscitation.
Clears heat and extinguishes wind.

Puncture:
With a 2 *cun* needle, at the opposite side of the painful part, puncture horizontally towards Yingxiang (Li 20) 迎香.

Technique:
From a standing position, hold the tip of the nose firmly. Insert the needle gently for about 1.5 *cun*. Stimulate the needle gently until pain occurs.

Get the patient to bend slowly forward, while turning the needle gently in a rotation similar to the motion of the patient.

Once the patient is bent to the maximum, ask the patient to come back to the straight position while you turn the needle gently the opposite way.

Repeat the procedure 2 or 3 times. The pain should disappear shortly afterwards.

Note:
This procedure is painful but very effective.

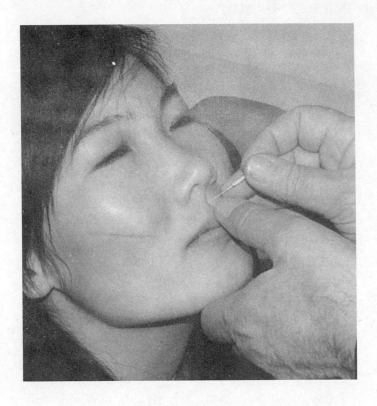

1. 急性腰椎痛

穴位：
人中亦称水沟－DU 26

特点：
开通闭塞，清热祛风。

用针：
采用 2 寸针，在腰椎痛部位的对侧向迎香穴（Li 20）水平运针。

方法：
采取站立位，紧紧握住鼻尖。缓缓进针 1.5 寸。轻轻用针刺激穴位，直至患者感到疼痛。

请患者慢慢向前弯腰，同时沿着患者运动的方向慢慢转动针。

当弯腰到最大幅度时，请患者回到直立位，同时向相反方向转动针。

在治疗中重复上述操作 2－3 次，随后疼痛会很快消失。

注：
这种方法虽然会使患者感到疼痛，但非常有效。

2. Acute Optic Neuritis

Point: 光明

Guangming — GB 37

Particularity:

Clears the liver and improves visual acuity. Reduces swelling and alleviates pain.

Itching and pain of the eyes, cataract, night blindness, optic atrophy and migraine

Puncture:

With a 2 *cun* needle, puncture perpendicularly up to 1.5 *cun*. Lift, thrust and rotate the needle, reducing manipulation to induce Qi. Retain the needle for 15 to 20 minutes.

2. 急性视神经炎

穴位：

光明－GB 37

特点：

清肝明目，消肿镇痛。

眼睛发痒、疼痛，白内障，夜盲症，青盲及偏头痛。

用针：

采用 2 寸针，垂直进针至 1.5 寸，提针、推针，然后转动针，降低运针幅度，使气导入。将针停留在穴位中 15—20 分钟。

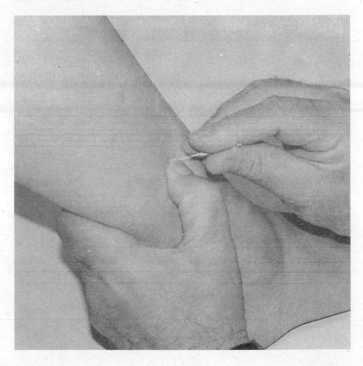

3. Acute Pharyngitis

Two Techniques are applicable.

(1) Bleeding the vein on the back of the ear

Choose the most prominent vein at the back of the ear. Scrape the area many times with the help of the nail to call the Qi. Prick the vein with a 3-edged needle while holding the vein between the thumb and index finger. Release few drops of blood and then stop the bleeding.

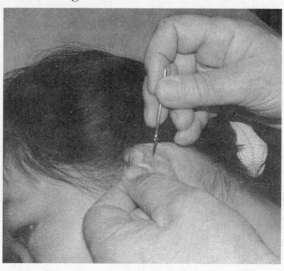

(2) Needling at the point 额中

Ezhong — extra point — point of the throat

On the middle line of the forehead, midway between Yintang 印堂 (extra point) and Shenting 神庭 (DU 24)

Puncture:

With a 1.5 *cun* needle, puncture the point Ezhong toward Yintang.

Technique:

Insert a needle up to ¾ of a *cun*. Lift and thrust for 20 seconds. Retain the needle for 30 minutes while the patient is resting in a horizontal position.

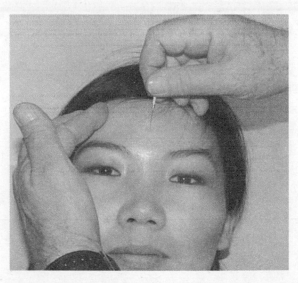

3. 急性咽炎

有两种治疗方法。

（1）耳背静脉放血：
在耳背上选择最明显的静脉。用指甲刮该区域多次，导通气脉。用拇指和食指捏住静脉，然后用三角针刺入静脉。放出几滴血之后停止放血操作。

（2）穴位针刺：
额中－奇穴－喉部穴位
在前额的中线上，在印堂（奇穴）和神庭（DU 24）之间的中点。

用针：
采用 1.5 寸针，向印堂方向刺额中穴。

方法：
进针至 3/4 寸，提针并推针 20 秒。将针停留在穴位内 30 分钟，其间患者水平体位休息。

4. Acute Conjunctivitis

Point: 耳尖

 The apex of the ear on the affected side

Puncture:

 Puncture the apex of the ear with a 3-edged needle, and squeeze out 3 to 5 drops of blood.

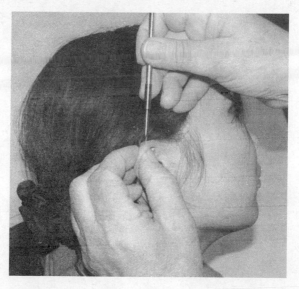

4. 急性结膜炎

穴位：

    患处一侧的耳尖

用针：

    用三角针刺耳尖，在耳尖处挤出 3－5 滴血。

5. Amenorrhea

Point: 上髎

Shangliao — UB 31

Puncture:

With a 1.5 *cun* needle, puncture perpendicularly in the sacral foramen.

Technique:

Try to identify the period of menstruation or choose a date when the woman feels "uncomfortable" or possibly "moody." The patient stands with her legs slightly apart and elbows resting on the table to allow her pubis and lower abdomen to be free from any compression.

Prior to the insertion of the needle, the practitioner should press the patient's abdomen 5 to 8 times with the fist, pushing slowly and releasing rapidly, to stimulate the uterus.

Insert the needle up to 1 *cun* into the point and twist the needle clockwise as far as possible.

Keep the needle that way until a contraction is felt

in the uterus. Perform the technique 3 times without removing the needle.

Both points should be stimulated.

Note:

The treatment should be repeated 25 days after the menstruation.

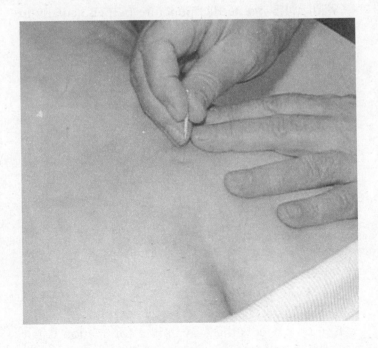

5. 闭经

穴位：

上髎—UB 31

用针：

采用 1.5 寸针，垂直刺入荐骨孔。

方法：

尽可能确定行经的时间。如果不能，建议选择女性感觉"不舒服"或可能感觉"心情不好"的日子。

让患者站在地上，双脚微微分开，把双肘放在桌上，使她的耻骨和下腹部不受任何挤压。

在进针之前，针灸师应握拳按压患者腹部 5—8 次。注意，按下时要缓，放开时要快，这样可以对子宫产生有效刺激。

在穴位处进针至 1 寸，沿顺时针方向捻针至最大幅度。

将针停留在该位置，直至患者感觉子宫收缩。

重复上述操作 3 次。

两个穴位都需要刺激。

注意：

月经后 25 天重复进行治疗。

6. Car and Air Sickness

Points: 安眠 1 and 安眠 2

Anmian 1 & Anmian 2 (extra points)

Anmian 1, at the midpoint between Yifeng (医风 Sj 17) and Yiming (医明 extra), situated in the sternocleidomastoid muscle, at the inferior border of the mastoid process, 1 *cun* posterior to Yifeng

Anmian 2, at the midpoint between Fengchi (风池 GB 20) and Yiming

Puncture:

With a 2 *cun* needle, puncture perpendicularly up to 1.5 *cun*. Thrust and rotate the needle gently. Apply to Anmian 1 and Anmian 2, one side only.

6. 晕车晕机

穴位：

安眠 1 和安眠 2（奇穴）

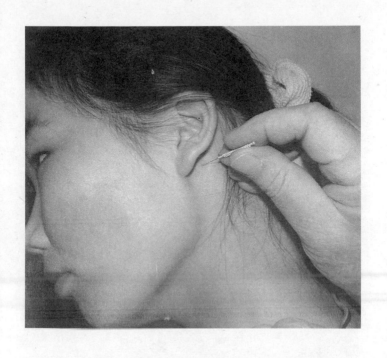

安眠 1 位于医风－SJ 17 和医明（奇穴）之间的中点，在胸锁乳突肌内，乳突的下缘，医风后面一寸。

安眠 2 位于风池－GB 20 和医明之间的中点。

用针：

采用 2 寸针，垂直进针 1.5 寸。轻轻推针并转动针。仅在一侧的安眠 1 和安眠 2 采用这种方法。

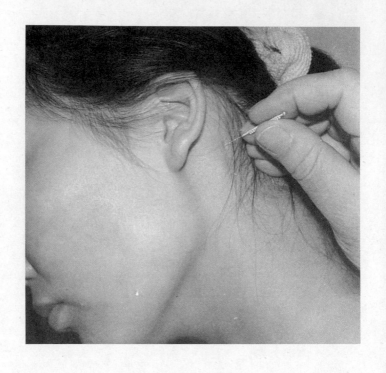

7. Coldness of the Extremities

Area:

The Coccyx

Particularity:

Unknown to many practitioners, this coccygeal therapy has tremendous healing effects. Years of research and practice show that the coccyx is one of the energy centres of the body, with the tip of the coccyx being the most energetic part and the first coccygeal vertebra being the least. The transverse process of the coccyx is rich in sensation, and therefore of importance to acupuncture in the treatment of many ailments.

Puncture:

Use a 1.5 *cun* needle, gauge 26, or a fine triangular needle.

Technique:

With the patient lying prone, insert the needle between the first coccygeal vertebra and the base of the sacrum. Thrust the needle up and down with mild stimulation. After removing the needle, repeat on both sides of the transverse process, the needle being orientated towards the exterior of the coccyx.

Another insertion of the needle is made at the mid point of the end and the top of the second coccygeal vertebra. The needle is stimulated by thrust and removed with or without retention.

The same can be applied with the triangular needle.

Note:
The treatment should last only a short period of time of plus-minus 5 minutes.

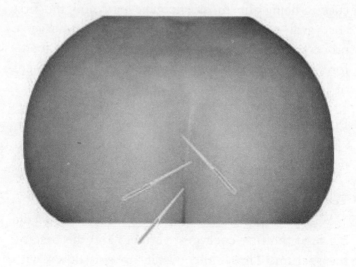

7. 四肢寒冷

部位：
 尾骨

特点：
 目前大多数针灸学家和针灸师一般都不知道有这种尾骨疗法。它具有显著的愈合能力，很多治疗手段都以这里为能量中心。

 多年来的理论研究和临床实践的结果都表明，尾骨是人体的主要活力中心之一。

 尾骨末端是能量最强的部分，而第一尾椎骨的能量最低。

 尾骨横突上遍布神经，因而在尾骨上进行针灸意义重大。

用针：
 采用 26 号 1.5 寸针，或三角针。

方法：
 请患者俯卧。

 在第一尾椎骨和骶骨底之间进针。上下推针，进行平缓刺激。取出针后，再在横突两侧重复该操作。针应朝向尾骨的外测。

另一种方法是在第二尾椎骨末端和顶端之间的中点进针。

通过推针来进行刺激，可以停留一段时间再取出，也可以直接取出。

采用三角针时，操作方法相同。

注意：

本疗法仅需要很短的时间，大约五分钟左右。

8. Constipation

Point: 秩边

    Zhibian — UB 54

Particularity:

    Clears the heat and removes dampness.

    Relieves swelling and cures hemorrhoids.

Puncture:

    Use a 4 *cun* needle.

Technique:

    Insert the needle 3 *cun* deep toward the perineum to induce a needling sensation.

    Retain the needle for 20 minutes. Stimulate only once after 10 minutes.

Note:

    In more acute case, 2 or 3 treatments may be required.

8. 便秘

穴位：
秩边—UB 54

特点：
清热除湿。
消肿通便。

用针：
采用 4 寸针。

方法：
进针至 3 寸深；推针至会阴，产生针感（得气）。
针停留 20 分钟，在 10 分钟后仅再刺激一次。

注意：
对于急性症，需要进行 2—3 次治疗。

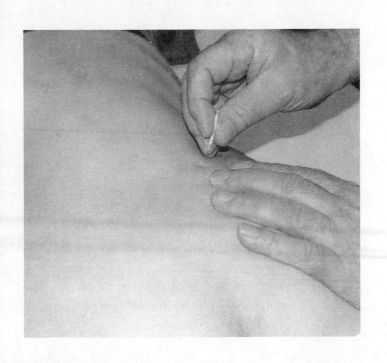

9. Cystitis and Urethritis

Point: 支沟
Zhigou — Sj 6

Puncture:
With a 2 *cun* needle, puncture perpendicularly.

Technique:
Insert the needle perpendicularly up to 1.5 *cun* deep.

Perform reinforcing and reducing to induce Qi. Retain the needle for up to 40 minutes.

Manipulating it every 10 minutes.

9. 膀胱炎

穴位：
支沟－Sj 6

用针:

采用 2 寸针,垂直运针。

方法:

垂直进针至 1.5 寸深。

通过加力和减力针刺,将气导入。

针停留达 40 分钟。

每 10 分钟运针一次。

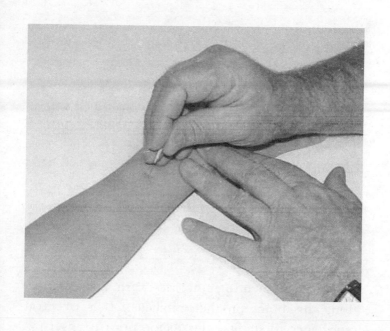

10. Enteritis

Point: 神阙

Shenque — CV 8

Particularity:

Warms and restores deteriorated *yang*.

Promotes urination and relieves Edema.

Puncture:

With a 1.5 *cun* needle, puncture perpendicularly.

Technique:

Insert the needle to a depth of 0.8 to 1 *cun* to induce Qi by a reinforcing manipulation. Remove the needle without retention.

Note:

Many acupuncture authorities warn against puncturing this point (in the umbilicus). It is of great importance to sterilize this region prior to insertion of the needle.

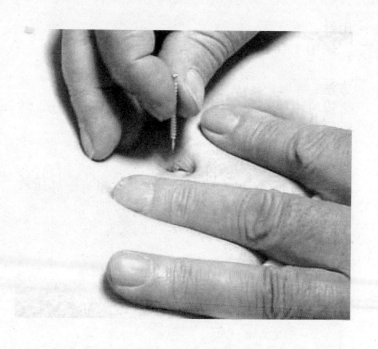

10. 肠炎

穴位:
神阙—CV 8

特点:
温补阳亏,利尿消肿。

用针：

采用 1.5 寸针，垂直运针。

方法：

进针 0.8 至 1 寸，通过加力运针将气导入，然后直接取出针，无需在穴内停留。

注意：

这是脐窝，针灸书籍的确规定不能对此处进行针刺。在进针前务必仔细对该部位消毒。

11. Epistaxis — Nosebleed

Points: 大敦 / 阴白

Dadun — Liv 1 and Yinbai — Sp 1

Technique:

Take a firm grip of the big toe of the foot on the opposite side of the bleeding nostril. Keep holding without releasing the pressure until the bleeding has stopped.

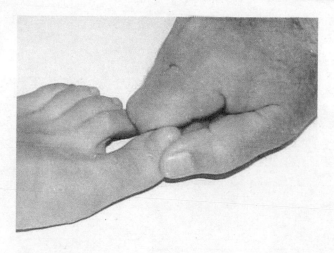

11. 鼻出血

穴位：

大敦—Liv 1 和阴白—Sp 1

方法：

紧握出血鼻孔另一侧的大脚趾。一直握住不放，直至鼻出血停止。

12. Gastrointestinal Neurosis

Points: 内关, 外关
Neiguan — Per 6,   Waiguan — TW 5

Puncture:

With a 2.5 *cun* or longer needle if needed, puncture perpendicularly into the point.

Technique:

Push the needle until the tip reaches the area under the skin at Waiguan.

Lift and thrust the needle quickly with small amplitude. While doing so, knead the abdomen gently for about 2 minutes.

While the patient takes deep breath, repeat the procedure after 5 minutes until the pain in the abdomen disappears.

Retain the needle for about 20 minutes.

12. 胃肠道功能紊乱

穴位：

内关－Per 6 至外关－TW 5

用针：

采用 2.5 寸针，必要时采用更长的针，垂直刺入穴位。

方法：

推针，直至针尖到达外关皮下区域。

小幅快速提针和推针，同时轻轻揉捏腹部约 2 分钟。

请患者深呼吸，5 分钟后重复上述操作，直至腹部疼痛消失。

将针停留 20 分钟左右。

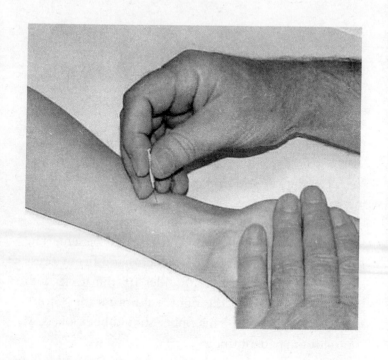

13. Headache

Points: 风池，胃舒

Fengchi — GB 20 (bilateral) and "Stomach Comfort," a new point discovered by the author, situated between the xiphoid process and the 7th rib

Technique:

Stand on the right side of the seated patient. The thumb and middle finger of the left hand firmly press the Fengchi points on both sides of the neck, with the middle finger of the right hand press the "Stomach Comfort" point. This finger should be hooked, as if to lift the patient up.

The pressure should be made in the same time by the 3 fingers. The patient should keep his/her head erect throughout the procedure, during which a woman patient should unfasten her bra.

Note:

This technique was developed by the author, and the headache should disappear within 15 seconds.

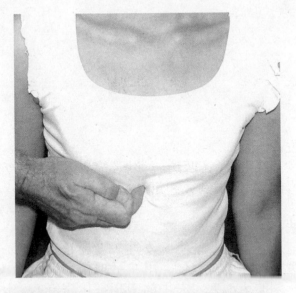

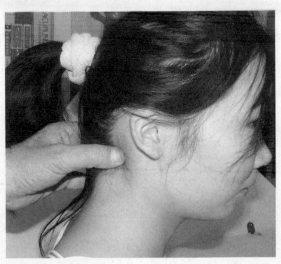

13. 头痛

穴位：

风池－GB 20（两边），以及笔者发现的新穴位"胃舒"，位于剑突和第七肋骨之间。

方法：

请患者坐在椅子上。女性患者应松开乳罩。

医师站在患者右侧。用左手拇指和中指紧按脖颈两侧的风池穴，右手的中指按压胃舒穴。这个手指形成勾状，好像要把患者从地上提起。

同时用三个手指进行按压。在整个治疗过程中，患者始终保持抬头姿势。

注：

这是作者发明的 15 秒疗法，保证 100％有效。不超过 15 秒钟患者就会感到头痛减轻。

14. Hiccup

Treatment One:

Point: 涌泉

Yongquan — K 1

Technique:

With the patient lying on the stomach, puncture the point Yongquan. Apply enough energy to stimulate the point until the hiccups cease. Remove the needle afterwards.

Note:

In severe cases, puncture the point bilaterally.

Treatment Two:

Points:

Middle of the thoracic vertebra, an area between the 3rd and 7th vertebra

Technique:

With the patient standing straight and pushing against a wall with both hands, press the tense areas on both

sides of the spine between the 3rd and 7th vertebrae. Maintain the pressure until the hiccups disappear.
Or:

While the patient lies on the stomach, apply the same technique as above.

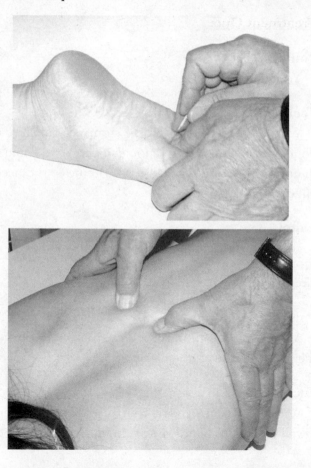

14. 呃逆

疗法 1:

穴位:
  涌泉－K1

方法:
  请患者俯卧,用拇指用力按压涌泉穴 1—2 分钟,对患者进行足够强度的刺激,直至患者停止呃逆。

注:
  对重症患者可针刺双脚涌泉穴。

疗法 2:

穴位:
  胸椎中部,在第 3 和第 7 椎骨之间。

方法:
  请患者直立在一面墙前,双手扶住墙。针灸师用双手拇指在第 3 和第 7 椎骨之间按压脊椎两侧最紧的部位,直至患者停止呃逆。
  用此疗法时患者也可俯卧。

15. Hysteria

(1) <u>Hysterical Mutism:</u>

Point: 涌泉
Yongquan — K 1

Puncture:
Use a 1.5 *cun* thick needle.

Technique:
Puncture Yongquan on one side up to ¾ of a *cun* deep. Thrust, lift and rotate the needle for about 3 minutes while you talk to the patient.

If the patient does not fully recover, puncture the other side.

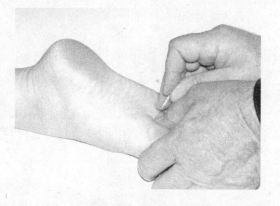

(2) <u>Hysterical Paralysis:</u>

Point: 环跳

Huantiao — GB 30

Puncture:

Use a 3.5 *cun*, gauge 28 needle.

Technique:

Insert the needle up to 3 *cun* deep toward the genitalia. Thrust and lift the needle with reducing manipulation for 3 minutes to induce numbness or even an electrical sensation radiating to the lower limbs. Remove the needle thereafter.

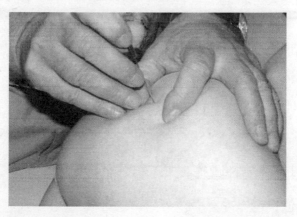

(3) <u>Hysterical Spasm:</u>

Point: 中脘

Zhongwan — Ren 12

Puncture:

Use a 2 *cun* needle.

Technique:

Insert the needle perpendicularly up to 1.5 *cun* deep. Perform a reducing manipulation with strong stimulation until the spasm stops.

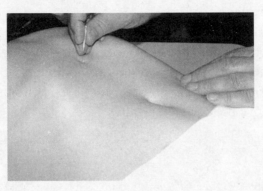

15. 癔病

（1）癔病性哑症

穴位：

涌泉—K 1

用针：

采用 1.5 寸粗针。

方法：
　　在一侧的涌泉穴进针到 3/4 寸深。推针、提针并转动针约 3 分钟，同时对患者说话。
　　如果患者未恢复说话功能，可以针刺另一侧。

（2）癔病性瘫痪

穴位：
　　环跳－GB 30

用针：
　　采用 28 号 3.5 寸针。

方法：
　　向生殖器进针到 3 寸深。推针、提针，逐渐减力，使下肢感到麻木，甚至有触电的感觉。
　　运针约 3 分钟，然后取出针。

（3）癔病性痉挛

穴位：
　　中脘－Ren 12

用针：
　　采用 2 寸针。

方法：
　　垂直进针到 1.5 寸。
　　减力运针，加强刺激，直至痉挛停止。

16. Impotence

Treatment One:

Point: 道门

Taomen — new point

(Located between the spinous process of C 3 and C 4)

This new point is an addition from the author.

Puncture:

Use a 1.5 *cun* thick needle.

Technique:

With the patient seated and the head bent slightly forward, puncture the point Taomen up to 1 *cun* deep with stimulation, lifting and thrusting. Retain the needle for 30 minutes, manipulating every 10 minutes.

Treatment Two:

Points: 尾骨

The tip of the coccyx and surrounding area.

Technique:

Insert the needle at the tip of the coccyx, using a fast thrusting and lifting technique, for about 15 seconds.

Then insert the needle in the surrounding parts of the coccyx with a quick thrusting and lifting technique, without retaining the needle.

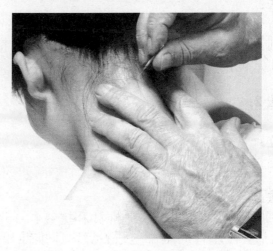

16. 阳痿

疗法 1：

穴位：
道门-新穴位

位于棘突 C 3 和 C 4 之间。

这是笔者发现的另一个新穴位。

用针：

采用 1.5 寸针。

方法：

请患者坐好，脖颈微微前弓。

刺针到 1 寸，进行刺激，提针、推针。将针停留在穴位内 30 分钟。每 10 分钟运针一次。

<u>疗法 2：</u>

穴位：

尾骨末端及周围。

方法：

在尾骨末端进针，快速推针和提针约 15 秒。

此后，在尾骨周围部位进针，快速推针和提针，不要将针停留。

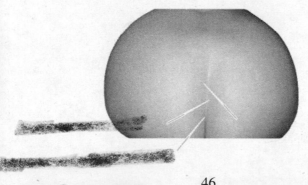

17. Insomnia

Points: 华佗夹脊

The Huatuojiaji points
(From the 1st cervical vertebra to the coccyx)

Puncture:

Use a 7 stars plum blossom hammer.

Technique:

First pinch the skin of the spine area with the thumb and index finger until the area is red. Then bleed the spine and the Huatuojiaji points to the coccyx with the plum blossom hammer. Let the patient rest for 30 minutes afterwards.

17. 失眠

穴位：
华佗夹脊
从第一颈骨到尾骨。

用针:

七星梅花锤。

方法:

准备:用拇指和食指用力掐脊椎部位的皮肤直至发红。

用梅花锤对脊骨和华佗夹脊穴位至尾骨放血。此后让患者休息 30 分钟。

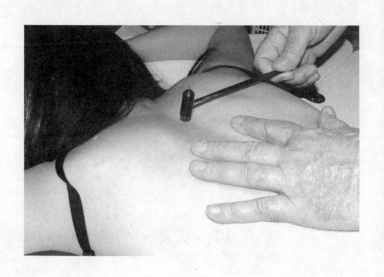

18. Intestinal Worms

Point: 至阴/指井
Zhiyin — UB 67

Puncture:
Use a 1 *cun* needle.

Technique:
Puncture perpendicularly at the new moon. Stimulate for about 1 minute. Retain the needle for about 40 minutes with a slight stimulation every 10 minutes.

18. 肠虫

穴位：
至阴亦称指井－UB 67

用针：
采用1寸针。

方法：

在新月时进行垂直针刺治疗，刺激约 1 分钟。将针停留在穴位中约 40 分钟，每 10 分钟轻微刺激一次。

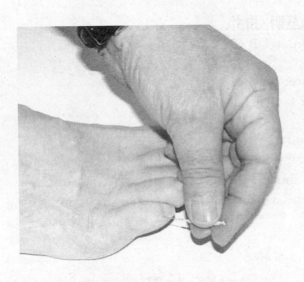

19. Nervous Tension

Points: 华佗夹脊

The Huatuojiaji points (from T 1 to S 1) plus the coccyx. Bilateral

Puncture:

Use a plum blossom hammer until some bleeding occurs.

Technique:

With the patient lying face downward, stimulate the back to activate Qi. Then stimulate with the plum blossom from the coccyx to the 1st thoracic vertebra. A 20 minutes rest is advisable following the treatment.

19. 神经紧张

穴位：

华佗夹脊穴，从 T 1 到 S 1，外加尾骨。两侧。

用针：

采用梅花锤，直至出血。

方法：

请患者俯卧。在开始治疗前刺激背部，调动气。用梅花锤从尾骨到第一胸椎进行刺激。建议患者在治疗后休息 20 分钟。

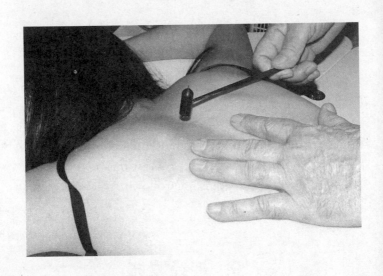

20. Painful Elevation of the Arm

Point: 外关
Waiguan — Sj 5

Puncture:
With a 2 *cun* needle, puncture perpendicularly in the opposite arm to the affected one.

Technique:
With the patient seated, insert the needle up to 1.5 *cun* deep in the opposite arm. Let the patient slowly raise the arm, while you turn the needle slowly but firmly in the direction of the motion of the arm (clockwise for the elevation and anti-clockwise for the lowering of the arm).

At the maximum elevation of the arm, hold the needle firmly for about 3 seconds. The patient should then lower the arm while the needle is turned in the opposite direction at the same speed as the arm.

Repeat the procedure 2 or 3 times until the affected arm is completely free of pain when elevated.

Note:

This technique is painful, but very effective.

20. 抬胳膊疼痛

穴位：

外关－Sj 5

用针：

采用 2 寸针，在患部的另一侧胳膊进行垂直针刺。

方法：

进针至 1.5 寸深。请患者坐着，慢慢向上抬起胳膊，此时针灸师沿手臂上举方向缓慢但有力地转动针。

当上举到最高处时，紧握针，不要松弛，保持 3 秒。然后请患者放下手臂，而针灸师以与手臂同样的速度反方向转动针。

重复上述操作 2－3 次，直至手臂运动自如。

注：

这种疗法会使患者感到疼痛，但非常有效。

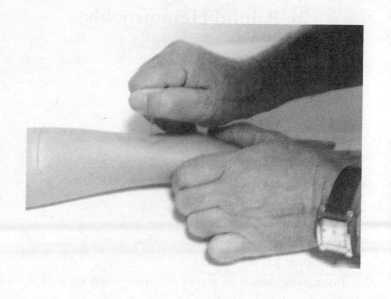

21. Painful Hemorrhoids

Point: 承山

Chengshan — UB 57

Puncture:

With a 2 *cun* needle, puncture perpendicularly to the skin.

Technique:

With the patient lying face downward, insert the needle up to 1.5 *cun* deep.

Rotate the needle at a very fast frequency of 300 to 350 times per minute to induce soreness, numbness and distention radiating to the popliteal fossa, lower leg and foot.

Retain the needle for 30 minutes, manipulating every 5 minutes.

21. 气海俞痛

穴位：
　承山－UB 57

用针：
　采用 2 寸针，垂直针刺皮肤。

方法：
　请患者俯卧，进针至 1.5 寸深。
　以很快的频率转针，1 分钟达 300－350 次，使酸胀和麻木的感觉一直放射到膝窝、小腿和脚部。
　将针停留 30 分钟。每 5 分钟运针一次。

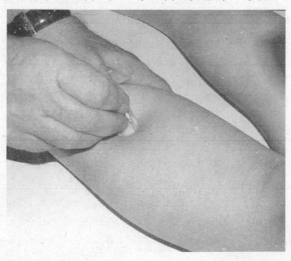

22. Painful Menstruation — Dysmenorrhea

Point: 上髎

Shangliao — UB 31 (in the first posterior sacral foramen)

Puncture:

With a 1.5 *cun* needle, puncture perpendicularly in the sacral foramen.

Technique:

With the patient leaning her elbows on a table, and with the feet slightly apart (the abdomen should not touch the table), insert the needle slowly up to 1 *cun* into the right sacral foramen. Twist the needle clockwise to its maximum and hold it in that position.

Put the other hand on the abdomen at the level of the uterus, without any compression, to send Qi from the hand holding the needle to the other hand.

A contraction in the uterus should be felt by the patient. Release the tension of the needle and wait for approximately 10 seconds before the second stimulation.

Note:

If the needle is difficult to extract as it may often be, use the second needle to extract it.

This is a very effective method developed by the author.

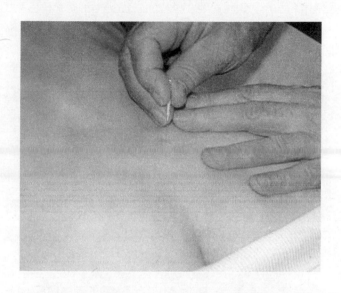

22. 痛经

穴位：

上髎－UB 31

位于第一后荐骨孔。

用针：

采用 1.5 寸针，垂直针刺荐骨孔。

方法：

患者站在地上，双脚微微分开。请她向前弯腰，将双肘放在桌子边上，腹部不要碰到桌子。

缓慢从右荐骨孔进针到 1 寸。顺时针捻针到极限位置，然后保持在这个位置，不要再动。

针灸师将另一只手放在患者腹部的子宫位置上，不要按压，将气从握针的一只手运到另一只手。

患者会感到子宫收缩。降低针刺的强度，等待约 10 秒钟，再进行下一次刺激。

注意：

经常会出现针被粘着在穴位内拔不出来。可以使用另一支针拔出来。

这是笔者发明的一种非常有效的治疗方法。

23. Smoking

Point: 天尾穴/率骨

(1) Tianweixue — extra point

Located on the hand, at the midpoint of the line connecting the points Lieque (L 7 列缺) and Yangxi (Li 5 阳溪)

(2) Shuaigu — GB 8

Puncture:

Use a 1 *cun* needle.

Technique:

Insert the needle perpendicularly 3-5 mm deep. At the same time, the patient should be breathing deeply. Manipulate the needle to induce Qi and create a sensation of numbness in the wrist or even in the arm.

The patient may experience a feeling of drowsiness or euphoria, and a metallic or other kind of taste in the mouth.

Retain the needle for 15-20 minutes.

Then insert the needle at Shuaigu (GB 8 率骨), downwards and towards the ear. Stimulate the needle until pain occurs, and then remove it.

23. 吸烟

穴位：
（1）天尾穴－奇穴
位于手上从列缺－L 7 到阳溪－Li 5 的连线的中点。
（2）率骨－GB 8

用针：
采用 1 寸针。

方法：
垂直进针 3－5mm 深，同时请患者深呼吸。运针，将气导入，使手腕甚至手臂有麻木感。

患者可能会有倦意或快感，但口中会感觉到有金属或其他味道。

将针停留在穴位中 15-20 分钟。这时可以在率骨（GB 8）进针。

向耳部进针，刺激直至有痛感，然后取出针。

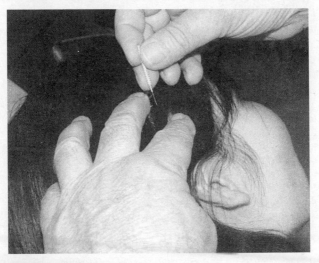

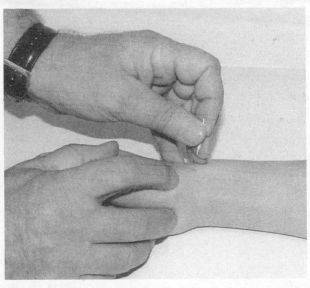

24. Stiff Neck

Point: 内关
Neiguan — Per 6

Puncture:
With a 1.5 *cun* needle, puncture perpendicularly on the same side as the pain, 1 to 1.2 *cun* deep.

Technique:
Rotate, lift and thrust the needle to induce Qi. Manipulate the needle for up to 5 minutes while the patient moves the neck.
Remove the needle.

24. 落枕

穴位：
内关－Per 6

用针：

采用 1.5 寸针。在患处一侧垂直针刺 1—1.2 寸深。

方法：

转动针，提针，推针，将气导入。运针 5 分钟，其间请患者转动脖颈。

此后取出针。

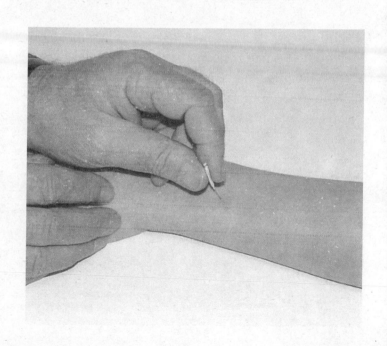

25. Stomach Ache

Point: 胃舒

"Stomach Comfort," situated between the xiphoid process and the 7th rib

Puncture:

With a 1.5 *cun* needle, puncture perpendicularly.

Technique:

With the patient lying face upward on a table, insert the needle perpendicularly at the right side of the xiphoid process.

Make a mild lift and thrust for about half a minute. Retain the needle for 30 minutes.

Note:

This procedure is not recommended in the case of pregnancy, as there is a possibility of causing contractions in the uterus.

25. 胃痛

穴位：

"胃舒"，位于剑突和第七肋骨之间。

用针：

采用 1.5 寸针，垂直刺针。

方法：

患者躺在桌上。在剑突右侧垂直进针。
轻轻提针和推针约半分钟。
将针停留在穴位内半小时。

注意：

此法对孕妇不宜。这可能会使子宫收缩。

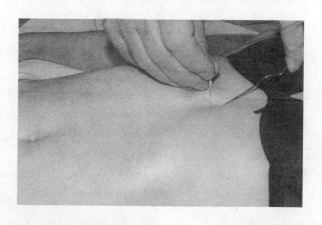

26. Tennis Elbow

Point: 阿是穴

Point Ashi

Particularity:

It is essential to locate and mark exactly the Ashi point on the affected tendon prior to insertion of the needle.

Puncture:

Use a 1 or 1.5 *cun* thick needle.

Technique:

Before inserting the needle, hold the tendon on both sides, so that it cannot move.

Insert a 1.5 *cun* needle at the Ashi point slowly towards the muscle.

The patient should feel a radiating pain. Thrust and lift the needle for about 1 minute. Then change the angle of penetration and thrust, and lift again as if intending to punish the tendon.

After about 2 or 3 penetrations at different angles, retain the needle for about 30 minutes.

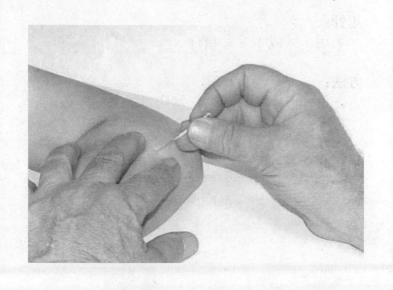

26. 网球肘

穴位：

阿是穴

特点：

在进行针灸之前，必须找准患处肌腱的阿是穴
位置并做出标记。

用针：

采用 1 寸或 1.5 寸粗针。

方法：

在进针前，要从两侧握紧肌腱，使之不能动。

将 1.5 寸针插入阿是穴，缓慢刺入肌肉。

患者会感到放射状疼痛。推针和提针约 1 分钟。然后改变刺入的角度，再次推针和提针，仿佛要进一步伤害肌腱。

从不同角度刺入 2—3 次，然后将针停留约半小时。

27. Toothache

Point: 掖门

Yemen — Sj 2

Puncture:

With a 1.5 *cun* needle, puncture obliquely towards the middle of the 4th and 5th carpal bones.

Technique:

Insert the needle up to 1 *cun* obliquely between the carpal bones. Rotate the needle to induce a needling sensation until the patient feels local soreness and distention radiating to the arm, elbow or fingertips. Retain the needle for 40 to 60 minutes.

If the pain persists, puncture the opposite site using the same stimulation.

27. 牙痛

穴位:

掖门—Sj 2

用针：

采用 1.5 寸针，斜着刺入第四和第五腕骨中间。

方法：

斜着进针到腕骨之间到 1 寸深。转动针，使患者产生针感，直至感觉到局部酸胀放射到手臂、肘部或指尖。将针停留在穴位内 40—60 分钟。

此后，如果牙疼未见缓解，针刺另一侧，进行同样的刺激。

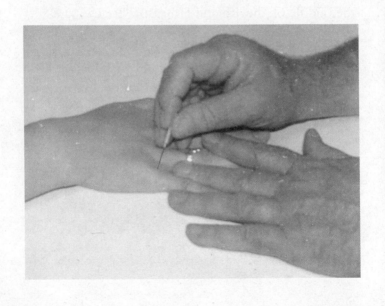

28. Vertigo

Same as for Car and Air Sickness (p. 14).

28. 眩晕

参见晕车晕机（14页）。

29. Vocal Chords Paralysis

(1) <u>Hysterical Aphasia</u>

Point: 涌泉
Yongquan — K 1

Puncture:
With a 1.5 *cun* thick needle, puncture perpendicularly.

Technique
Insert the needle perpendicularly into the point. Lift and thrust, then rotate vigorously for 1-10 minutes. The ability to speak should return in the course of treatment.

(2) <u>Vocal Chord Paralysis</u>

Point: 内关
Neiguan — Per 6

Puncture:
Puncture perpendicularly, with a 1.5 *cun* needle.

Technique:

Insert the needle perpendicularly up to 1 *cun*. Lift and thrust while rotating the needle to induce strong stimulation for about 5 minutes.

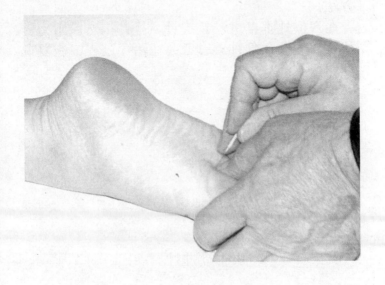

29. 声带麻痹症

（1）癔病性失语症：

穴位：
涌泉—K 1

用针：

采用 1.5 寸针，垂直刺针。

方法：

在穴位处垂直进针。提针、推针，然后用力转动针约 1—10 分钟。患者会在治疗过程中恢复说话能力。

（2）声带麻痹症：

穴位：

内关—Per 6

用针：

垂直刺针。采用 1.5 寸针。

方法：

垂直进针 1 寸。提针、推针，同时转动针，进行强力刺激约 5 分钟。

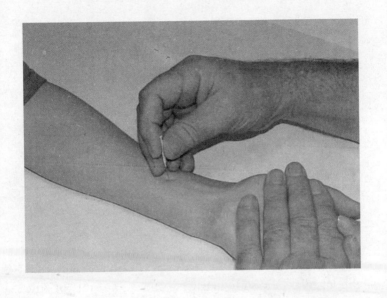

30. Vomiting

Point: 胃舒

"Stomach Comfort" (situated between the xiphoid process and the 7th rib)

Puncture:

Puncture perpendicularly with a 1.5 *cun* needle.

Technique:

With the patient lying face upward on a table, insert the needle perpendicularly at the right side of the xiphoid process.

Gently lift and thrust for about half a minute.

Then retain the needle for 30 minutes.

30. 呕吐

穴位：

胃舒，位于剑突和第七肋骨之间。

用针：

采用 1.5 寸针，垂直刺针。

方法：

患者躺在桌子上。在剑突右侧垂直进针。

轻轻提针和推针约半分钟。

将针停留半小时。

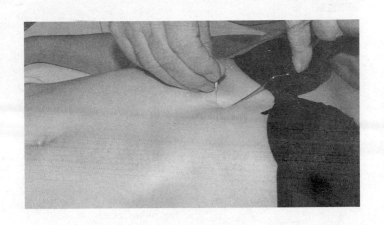

图书在版编目（ＣＩＰ）数据

一根针，一种治疗 /（比）金科煜著. —北京: 外文出版社, 2006
ISBN 7-119-04441-9

Ⅰ. 一... Ⅱ. 金... Ⅲ. 针灸疗法 —英、汉 Ⅳ. R245

中国版本图书馆 CIP 数据核字（2006）第 045094 号

责任编辑	郁 苓	
封面设计	金科煜	王 志
插图绘制	金科煜	
排版设计	李 耀	
印刷监制	张国祥	

一根针，一种治疗

金科煜 著

*

© 外文出版社

外文出版社出版
（中国北京百万庄大街 24 号）
邮政编码 100037
外文出版社网址: http://www.flp.com.cn
外文出版社电子信箱: info@flp.com.cn
sales@flp.com.cn

三河市汇鑫印务有限公司印刷
中国国际图书贸易总公司发行
（中国北京车公庄西路 35 号）
北京邮政信箱第 399 号 邮政编码 100044

2006 年(34 开)第 1 版
2006 年第 1 版第 1 次印刷
（英汉）
ISBN 7-119-04441-9
02100(平)
14-EC-3715P